YOUR BEDROOM IS a SOLAR SYSTEM!

Bring Outer Space Home with Glow-in-the-Dark Stickers of the Sun, Moon, Planets, and Stars!

HANNAH SHELDON-DEAN

WHALEN
BOOK · WORKS

Kennebunkport, Maine

13-digit ISBN: 978-1-95151-101-2
10-digit ISBN: 1-95151-101-8

This book may be ordered by mail from the publisher. Please include $5.99 for postage and handling. Please support your local bookseller first!

Books published by Whalen Book Works are available at special discounts when purchased in bulk. For more information, please email us at info@whalenbookworks.com.

Whalen Book Works
68 North Street
Kennebunkport, ME 04046

www.whalenbookworks.com

Cover and interior design by Melissa Gerber
Typography: Andes Bold, Andes, Book, Adobe Caslon, Allspice Alternates Regular, Allspice Regular, Canvas Curly Sans Combined, Conduit ITC Bold, Fontbox Boathouse Filled Regular, Futura, Handegypt, Hank BT, Times New Roman, Wayfarer

Printed in China
1 2 3 4 5 6 7 8 9 0

First Edition

DEDICATED TO
STARGAZERS
EVERYWHERE

Contents

A MAP OF OUR SOLAR SYSTEM AND BEYOND 6

OUR LITTLE CORNER OF THE UNIVERSE 7

OUR AMAZING SOLAR SYSTEM 8

THE SUN 10

THE EIGHT PLANETS 12

DWARF PLANETS 22

MOONS 24

ASTEROIDS, COMETS, AND METEORS 32

BEYOND OUR SOLAR SYSTEM 34

THE STARS 35

GALAXIES 40

BLACK HOLES 42

EXPLORING SPACE 43

SPACECRAFT 45

LOOKING FOR LIFE OUT THERE 48

THE KUIPER BELT 50

THE OORT CLOUD 51

DARK MATTER 52

GLOSSARY 54

HOW TO STICKER YOUR ROOM 58

STICKERS 61

a map of OUR SOLAR SYSTEM

AND BEYOND

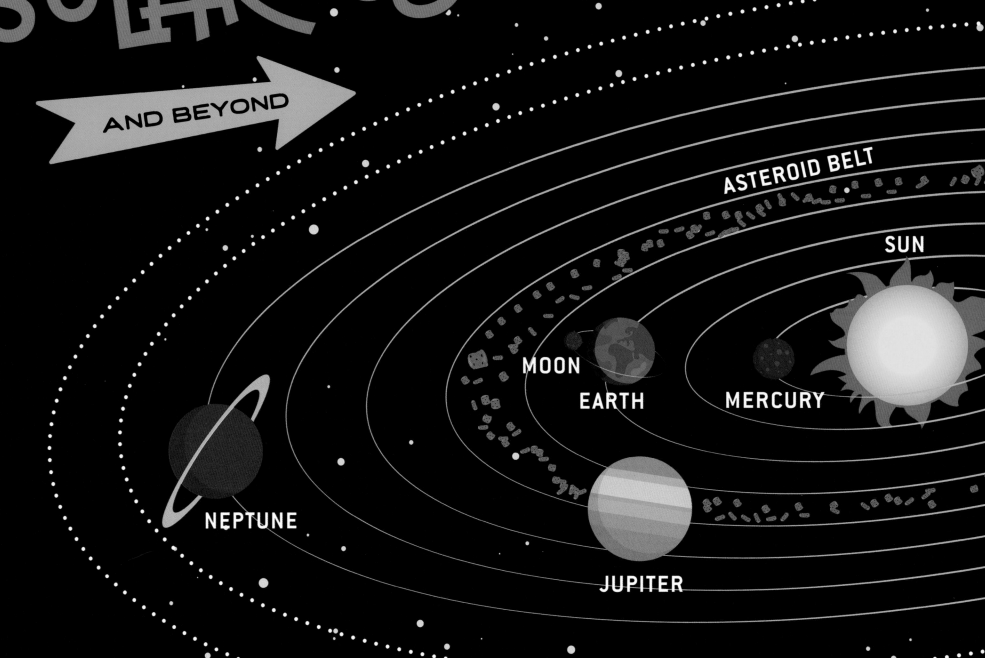

ASTEROID BELT

SUN

MOON

EARTH

MERCURY

NEPTUNE

JUPITER

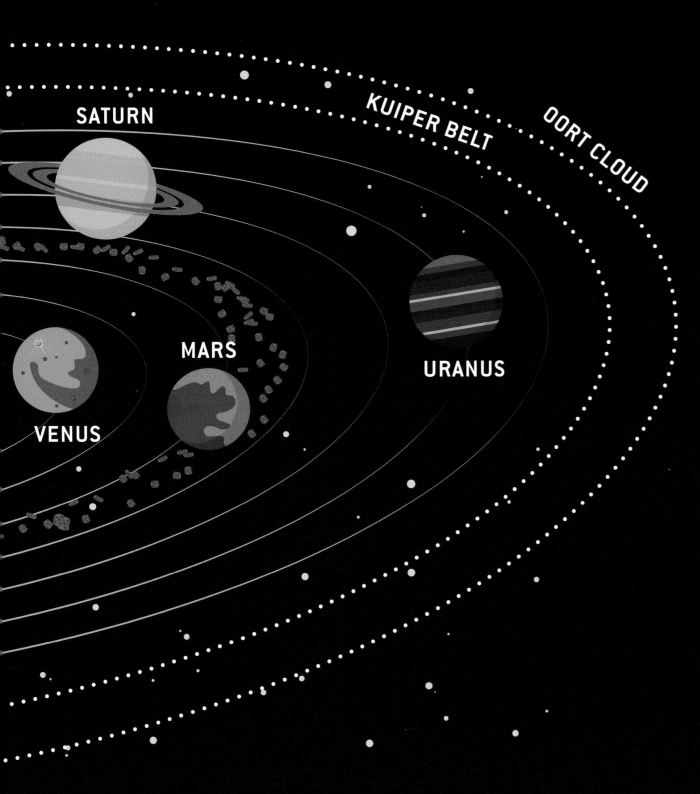

SATURN

KUIPER BELT

OORT CLOUD

MARS

URANUS

VENUS

Welcome to our solar system! Our solar system is one of countless solar systems in **the Milky Way,** our home galaxy. Each solar system has at least one star at its center—ours is **the Sun!** Everything in our solar system is held together by the Sun's gravity.

The eight known planets in our solar system—including our home planet, Earth!—all move around the Sun in what's called an orbit. The circles on this map represent the planets' different orbits—notice that some planets are much closer to the Sun, but they all move around it.

Other than the Sun, the planets are the biggest things in our solar system. But it's home to lots of other interesting things, too! There are the **moons** around many of the planets. There are the **asteroids, comets, and meteors** that fly through space, including the ones in the enormous **asteroid belt** between Jupiter and Mars. There are **dwarf planets,** too, plus lots of mysterious **dark matter** and **dark energy** that scientists don't fully understand yet.

Way out past Neptune is the distant, icy region known as the **Kuiper Belt**. And even farther than that, there's the **Oort Cloud**, which scientists think goes around the whole solar system like a bubble. And who knows? There might even be other living things somewhere in our solar system!

SOLAR SYSTEM

NEPTUNE

Windy, icy, and enormous, Neptune is farther away from Earth than any other planet in our solar system. Neptune's gaseous atmosphere makes it look blue, but it's so far away that it can't be seen from Earth by the naked eye.

SATURN

Gas giant Saturn is the second-largest planet in our solar system. It's famous for its beautiful rings, which are made up of pieces of rock and ice.

URANUS

Uranus is a massive ice giant. It has thirteen rings, and it's the only planet in our entire solar system that spins on its side instead of upright.

JUPITER

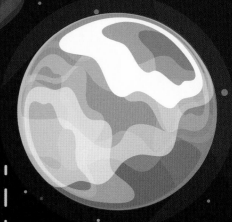

Jupiter is by far the biggest planet in our solar system. Jupiter is a gas giant, and the Great Red Spot on its surface is actually an enormous storm made of gaseous clouds.

MARS

Often called the Red Planet, Mars is cold, rocky, and about half the size of Earth. It's been visited by many spacecraft from Earth, including rovers that have explored its surface.

VENUS

Venus is closer to Earth than any other planet. It is the hottest planet in our solar system, and while most planets spin from west to east, Venus rotates the opposite way.

EARTH

Our home! Unlike any other planet in our solar system, Earth has liquid water on its surface, which makes it a great place for life to thrive.

MERCURY

The smallest planet in our solar system, Mercury is also the closest to the Sun. Mercury spins slowly, but it moves through its orbit around the Sun faster than any other planet.

SUN

The Sun is our home star, and its energy is the source of all life on Earth. Like other stars, it is made up of hot gas. The Sun's gravity holds everything in our solar system together.

the SUN

OUR ONLY STAR

The Sun is a very big, very hot ball of gas. Its gravity is the thing that holds the entire solar system together—we wouldn't have a solar system at all without it! Even though we call it by a special name, the Sun is actually a star—there are billions more like it in the Milky Way galaxy alone.

Our Sun's Vital Stats:

Age:
About 4.5 billion years

Core Temperature:
About 27 million degrees Farenheit

Surface Temperature:
About 10 thousand degrees Farenheit

Distance from Earth:
92.92 million miles

SUNSPOTS
Sometimes, the surface of the sun looks like it has dark spots on it. These darker areas are called **sunspots**. Sunspots show up in places where the sun's magnetic activity is greater, which can make the surface temperature lower in those places.

HANDLE WITH CARE

The sun gives off waves of three major kinds of energy. The first two are **heat** and **visible light**. Even in the coldest parts of the world, and even at night, the sun's energy is what keeps us warm enough to live! The third kind of energy is called **ultraviolet light**. We can't see ultraviolet light with just our eyes, but it can burn our skin—that's where sunburns come from.

MASS MATTERS

Compared to some even larger stars, the Sun isn't all that big. But compared to Earth and everything on it, the Sun is enormous! For example, the Sun is over 2,700,000 miles around at its equator. The Earth is just under 25,000 miles around at its equator. Plus, the Sun has much more **mass** than anything else in our solar system. Put simply, mass is a way of talking about how much **matter** there is in something—how much physical *stuff* something holds. The Sun's mass makes up 99.8% of *all* the mass in the whole solar system!

HOT STUFF

There are many different kinds of stars. Our Sun is what's called a **yellow dwarf star**, which is a medium-sized star. Sometimes, yellow dwarf stars are actually white—and that's true of our Sun, too! It just looks yellow to us because we see it through the gasses in our atmosphere. The hottest part of the Sun is the core at its center, which is an especially dense ball of burning gas. The temperature gets cooler in the outer layers of the Sun, but at its surface, the Sun is still hot enough to make diamonds boil!

THE EiGHT PLANETS

ORBITING OUR STAR

Another thing that's different for different planets is their **rotation**. All planets turn on an imaginary line called on axis, which runs through the middle of the planet like the core of an apple. When a planet spins around once on its axis, that's one rotation. The time it takes for a planet to complete one rotation is the length of a day on that planet—for us on Earth, one rotation takes twenty-four hours!

WONDERFUL WORLDS

The eight known planets are the biggest things in our solar system besides the Sun itself. But what exactly is a planet? It's not an easy question to answer! Scientists have argued about the definition of a planet since ancient times. But in 2006, the International Astronomical Union (a big group of scientists from around the world) decided that all planets have to do three things:

1. They have to orbit a star. (In our solar system, that's the Sun!)

2. They have to be big enough that their gravity forces them into the shape of a ball.

3. They have to be the only very large objects near their orbits around the Sun.

Planets have those three things in common, but in other ways they're very different! In our solar system, there are three kinds of planets: **rocky planets** (Mercury, Venus, Earth, and Mars), **gas giants** (Jupiter and Saturn), and **ice giants** (Uranus and Neptune). The rocky planets are sometimes called the "inner planets" because they're closer to the Sun, and the rest are the "outer planets."

PLANETARY PARTICULARS

Some planets have **rings** around them; others don't. Some planets have **moons** that orbit them; others don't. Some planets are enormous, while others are small—Jupiter is almost 30 times as wide as Mercury! The incredible variety among the planets is part of what makes our solar system such a fascinating place.

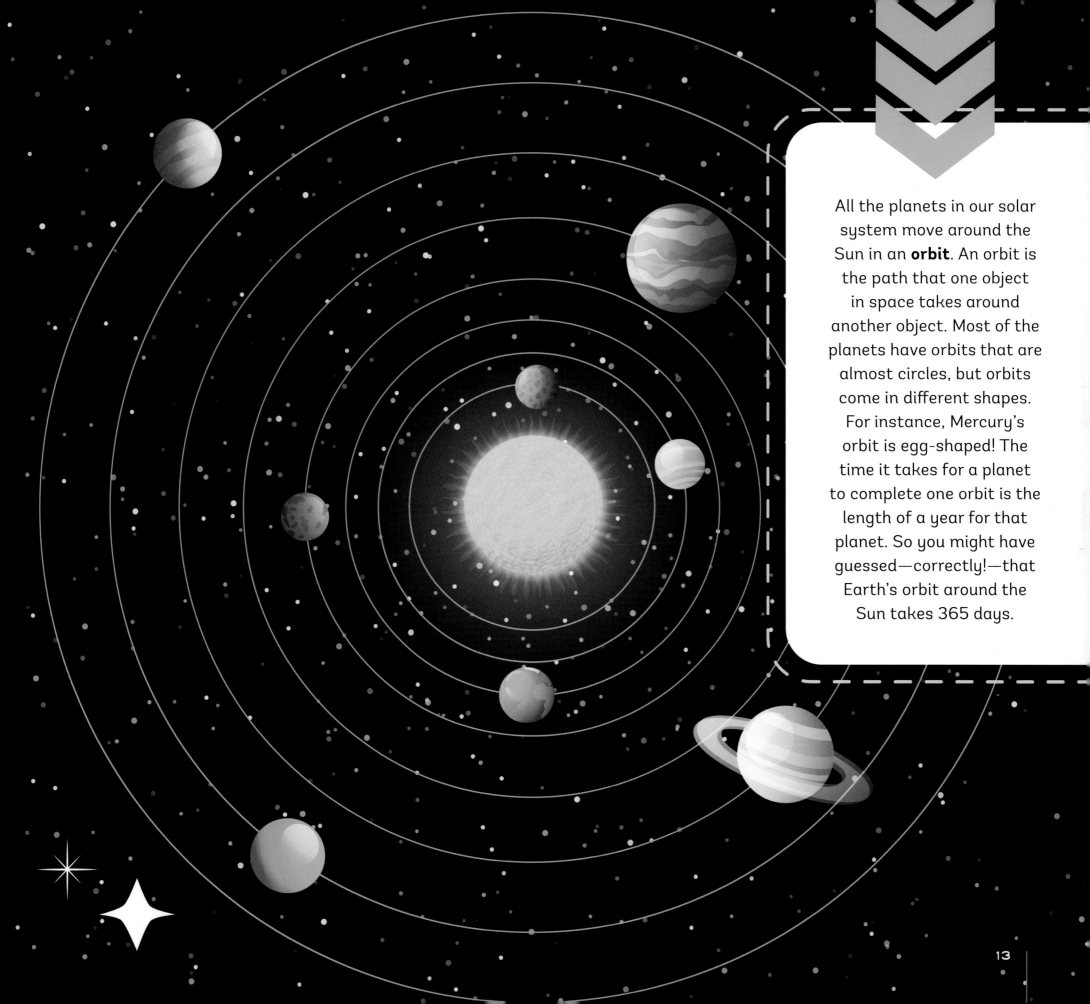

All the planets in our solar system move around the Sun in an **orbit**. An orbit is the path that one object in space takes around another object. Most of the planets have orbits that are almost circles, but orbits come in different shapes. For instance, Mercury's orbit is egg-shaped! The time it takes for a planet to complete one orbit is the length of a year for that planet. So you might have guessed—correctly!—that Earth's orbit around the Sun takes 365 days.

MERCURY

SPACE SPEEDER

Mercury is named after a famously fast god from Roman mythology. That's because it's the speediest of the planets—following an egg-shaped **orbit**, it makes a full trip around the Sun in only 88 Earth days. Many of the craters on Mercury's rocky surface are named after writers, artists, and musicians. There's even a colorful crater named for Dr. Seuss!

Mercury is the smallest planet (just a little bit bigger than Earth's moon), and it's the closest to the Sun. If you were to stand on Mercury and look at the Sun, it would look more than three times as big as it looks from Earth!

Venus

A WILD WORLD

Things are never dull on Venus! It features enormous volcanoes and tall mountains, and acidic clouds blow across its surface powered by winds as strong as hurricanes. Some scientists even think that there may once have been water on Venus's surface. Venus is named for the Roman goddess of beauty and love.

Because Venus is so close to the Sun, a year there only lasts 225 Earth days. But Venus spins very slowly—one Venus day is equal to 243 Earth days. That's right: each Venus day lasts longer than a full Venus year.

CAN YOU TAKE THE HEAT?

Venus is the hottest planet in our solar system, even though Mercury is closer to the Sun. That's because Venus has a dense **atmosphere** made up mostly of carbon dioxide, and all that thick gas keeps heat trapped close to the planet. The temperature on Venus is higher than 800 degrees Farenheit!

EARtH

OUR OWN HOME

Earth isn't just humans' home. It's also the home of all the living things in our solar system—as far as we know, anyway! One of the reasons that Earth is unique is that its air is perfect for creatures like us to breathe—78% nitrogen, 21% oxygen, plus very small amounts of other gases. About 4.5 billion years ago, Earth formed out of clouds of dust and gas that were pulled together by gravity. The other planets are named after ancient Roman or Greek gods, but not Earth—its name comes from English and German words that just mean "the ground."

SEASONS IN SPACE

On Earth, the seasons each year happen because of our planet's tilted **axis**. Because Earth spins at an angle, the Northern Hemisphere is tilted toward the Sun during one part of the year, while the Southern Hemisphere is tilted toward the Sun during a different part of the year. This unequal heat from the Sun is what gives us different seasons throughout the year!

WATER WORLD

Earth has a rocky surface, but it's also considered an **ocean planet**. That's because water covers about 70% of Earth's surface! In fact, Earth is the only planet in our solar system that has liquid water on it surface, which is a big part of why it's such a good place for life to thrive.

MARS

THE RED PLANET

Mars is a chilly desert planet covered in rocks, canyons, and dead volcanoes. It's named after the ancient Roman god of war, because the planet's red surface looks like it could be covered in blood. But really, Mars looks red to us because its soil contains a lot of iron, which turns red when it touches the oxygen in Mars's atmosphere. In other words, Mars is just rusty!

Mars has a lot of interesting landmarks on its surface, but one of the most exciting is a volcano called **Olympus Mons**. Olympus Mons is three times taller than Mt. Everest! And if its base were on Earth, it would be big enough to cover the entire state of New Mexico. Even though it probably hasn't erupted in millions of years, Olympus Mons is the largest volcano in the entire solar system.

RED ROVERS

Scientists believe that billions of years ago, Mars may have been a very different place. Long ago, Mars could have had a warmer climate and liquid water—perhaps even living creatures!

Scientists know all this thanks to the many spacecraft that have explored Mars over the years. Some of them orbit Mars to study it from afar, while some spacecraft—called **rovers**—land on the surface of the planet itself.

Other than Earth, Mars is the planet that humans have been able to study the most. That's because it's relatively close to Earth and has a rocky surface that spacecraft can land on.

JUPITER

Days on Jupiter are quick: it only takes about 10 Earth hours for Jupiter to make one full rotation. But on the other hand, it takes Jupiter a long time to orbit the Sun, which means that years on Jupiter are much longer than years on Earth. One Jupiter year is equal to about 12 Earth years!

THE GREAT RED SPOT

Jupiter is famous for its **Great Red Spot**. It may look like the spot is always the same, but in fact, it's changing all the time—because it's actually an enormous storm! The Great Red Spot is bigger than the entire Earth, and the storm has been going on for hundreds of years. Like other storms on Jupiter (and the rest of the planet's surface), it's made out of windswept clouds.

KING OF THE PLANETS

Jupiter is the biggest planet in our solar system—by a lot! Jupiter is more than twice as massive as all of the other planets in our solar system *put together*. Or, think of it this way: measured across its equator, Jupiter is as wide as 11 Earths put together. But even though it's huge, Jupiter isn't solid. It's a **gas giant**, which means that instead of a solid surface like Earth's or Mars's, it has a swirling, misty surface made of gas and liquid. Jupiter also has over 75 moons, and it is named after the ancient Roman god who was known as the king of all the other gods.

A GLORIOUS GIANT

Like Jupiter, Saturn is a **gas giant**—it doesn't have a solid surface, and it's mostly made of hydrogen and helium. Saturn is also huge! It's the second-biggest planet in our solar system. If you lined up nine Earths next to each other, they would almost be as wide as Saturn—and that's not including its famous rings.

Saturn

Of all the fascinating things about Saturn, it's most famous for its incredible **rings**. It has seven beautiful rings, and they reach as far as 175,000 miles away from Saturn itself.

The rings sometimes look solid, but they're made of billions of bits of floating rock and ice. Scientists think that these bits used to be pieces of comets, asteroids, and other space rocks before they got pulled apart by Saturn's gravity.

Some of the pieces of ice and rock in Saturn's rings are as tiny as grains of sand (or even tinier!), but some of them are much, much bigger. Some pieces are as big as a car or a house—and a couple are the size of mountains!

MANY MOONS

Saturn is famous for its moons, too. There are over 50 that have already been discovered, plus at least 20 more that scientists are still working on confirming. Saturn's name comes from the ancient Roman god of farming and wealth.

URANUS

SIDE SPINNER

The most unusual thing about Uranus is its **rotation**. Like Venus, it rotates from east to west—the opposite direction from most of the planets! Plus, Uranus is the only planet that spins on its side. That gives Uranus very extreme seasons, because the Sun shines directly on one end of the planet for so long. When that happens, it's winter on the other half of the planet—for 21 Earth years straight!

A FROZEN WORLD

Uranus is a freezing cold planet that was the first one in our solar system to be discovered using a telescope. It's about four times as wide as Earth and it has 13 rings, although its rings are harder to see than Saturn's rings. Uranus has lots of moons—27 in total!—and they're all named after characters from literature. Most of their names (like Juliet!) come from William Shakespeare's plays. Uranus itself is named after the Greek god of the sky.

ICE GIANTS

Both Uranus and Neptune are known as **ice giants**, which means that their surfaces are made of a foggy mixture of methane, ammonia, and water. The methane is what makes both planets look blue! Underneath, Uranus and Neptune each have a smaller core made of rock. Since they're so cold and far away from Earth, neither planet has ever been studied up close by humans. **Voyager 2** flew by Uranus and Neptune on its way out of our solar system, but no other spacecraft has visited them.

Neptune

WINDY WORLD

Neptune is farther away from the Sun than any other planet in our solar system. It's only a little smaller than Uranus, but unlike all the other planets, it's so far away that it can't even be seen with the human eye alone—we have to use telescopes to look at it. Neptune is cold, dark, and extremely windy! It's covered in clouds made of frozen methane, which blow around in winds about five times as strong as the strongest winds on Earth. The winds on Neptune move almost as fast as a fighter jet! Neptune also has a few faint rings that are difficult to see.

• RULER OF THE OCEAN •

Neptune has 14 moons, and all of them are named after sea deities and water nymphs from Greek myths. That's appropriate because Neptune itself is named after the Roman god of the ocean. Neptune is in good company, too—in mythology, his brothers are Jupiter and Pluto!

THE DWARF PLANETS

SMALL BUT MIGHTY →

Five Mini Planets and Counting

Dwarf planets are round like planets and orbit the Sun like planets, but they're much smaller. Because they have less **mass**, their gravity isn't strong enough to clear other large objects out of their **orbits**. But dwarf planets aren't moons—they orbit the Sun itself rather than other planets.

So far, scientists have found five dwarf planets in our solar system, but there could be at least 100 more that haven't been discovered yet!

CERES

Ceres is a huge rocky object in the asteroid belt between Mars and Jupiter, which means it's the closest dwarf planet to Earth. It used to be called an asteroid, but scientists classified it as a dwarf planet in 2006 because it's so much bigger than the other asteroids in the belt. Ceres is much smaller than Earth, but it has something in common with our home: water! There seems to be water vapor and ice on Ceres, so scientists hope to search there for signs of life.

PLUTO

Pluto is smaller than Earth's moon, but until 2006 it was classified as the ninth planet in our solar system. Pluto is still a fascinating world full of unusual geology. It's icy and freezing cold, it has enormous mountains, and there's even snow. But on Pluto, the snow is red! Pluto was named for the Roman god of the underworld. The person who gave Pluto its name might surprise you: it was an 11-year-old English girl, who suggested the name to her grandfather. He passed the idea on to the astronomers who discovered the dwarf planet, and it stuck!

PLANET X The Hypothetical Planet

In addition to the eight planets and five dwarf planets discovered in our solar system so far, there's also Planet X. Planet X isn't technically a planet—not yet, anyway! Some scientists think that because of the way some of the objects in the **Kuiper Belt** move, there might be a hidden object with a strong gravitational force somewhere nearby. If it's real, that object is Planet X! It would be about the size of Neptune, and it would exist way out past Pluto—much farther from the Sun than any other planet in our solar system.

MAKEMAKE

Makemake was discovered in 2005. It's named after a god of the Rapa Nui people, who live on Easter Island in the Pacific Ocean. Like Eris, Haumea, and Pluto, Makemake is in the **Kuiper Belt**. It's a cold, rocky world.

HAUMEA

Named after a Hawaiian goddess, Haumea is another dwarf planet in the Kuiper Belt. It's also about the same size as Pluto, and it's another icy, distant world. What's exciting about Haumea is its spin! It rotates faster than most other large objects in our solar system, and the fast spin makes it look like a football—even though it's really round.

ERIS

Eris was discovered in 2003, and it's about the same size as Pluto. Eris was one of the discoveries that led scientists to create the new classification of dwarf planet. Eris's name comes from the Greek goddess of conflict—which makes sense, since scientists had a lot of disagreement about how to classify dwarf planets!

Moons

There are more than 150 moons in our solar system!

Only 24 people have ever visited the Moon, and of those, just half got to walk on its surface. But humans have sent more than 100 robotic spacecraft to explore the Moon—including three that are studying it right now!

EARTH'S MOON

OUR NEAREST NEIGHBOR

Scientists think that the Moon was formed billions of years ago when an object the size of Mars smashed into Earth. Now, our moon orbits Earth, and it's the only other place in the solar system that human beings have visited in person. The Moon's surface is rocky and covered with craters, mountains, and valleys. On the Moon, gravity is only about one-sixth as strong as it is on Earth!

There are over 150 moons in our solar system, but until Galileo discovered four of Jupiter's moons in 1610, no one knew about all those other moons. That's why ours is just called "the Moon." It's the fifth-largest moon in the solar system.

CLIMATE CONTROL

The Moon plays a huge role in shaping the climate on Earth. Because of the Moon's gravitational pull, the Earth is more stable on its axis, which means that things like temperature and weather stay more stable too—and humans have an easier time living here! The Moon's gravity is also what causes the ocean's steady tides.

Warrior Moons

Mars has two moons, **Phobos** and **Deimos**. They're named after the mythological sons of Ares, the Greek god of war (the Greek version of the Roman god Mars!). Phobos and Deimos are both quite small compared to many of the other moons in our solar system. They're both made of a mixture of rock and ice, which scientists think might mean that they were once asteroids that got caught in Mars's gravity.

DEIMOS

Deimos is the smaller of Mars's two moons. Deimos has a lumpy surface with some craters, but it doesn't have any giant craters or grooves like Phobos. Someday, scientists might try to use Deimos or Phobos as bases to examine Mars from. That's because the moons are close enough from the planet that they could launch **rovers** between them.

PHOBOS

Phobos is bigger than Deimos. It is most notable for the enormous crater on its surface, which is called **Stickney**. Stickney is six miles wide! Phobos also has long grooves across its surface, like giant scratch marks. Phobos's **orbit** around Mars is a spiral, which means that it is always moving a tiny bit closer to Mars. So within about 50 million years, it could crash into Mars. Or, it might break into pieces and become a ring around Mars.

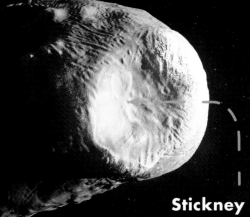

Stickney Crater

NEVER GIVE UP

Both Phobos and Deimos were discovered in 1877. The astronomer who was searching for them almost quit trying, but his wife encouraged him to keep going and he discovered Deimos the next night!

JUPITER'S MOONS

Giants, Volcanoes, and Hidden Oceans

Jupiter has at least 79 moons! So far, scientists have named 53 of them. The four largest of Jupiter's moons were discovered a long time ago, in 1610. In fact, they were the first moons ever discovered beyond Earth's moon. Because Italian astronomer Galileo Galilei discovered them, these four moons are called the Galilean satellites: **Io**, **Europa**, **Ganymede**, and **Callisto**.

GANYMEDE

Ganymede is the biggest moon in our whole solar system. It's even larger than Mercury! Ganymede is also the only moon that has it own magnetic field, which creates streams of glowing gas over its icy surface.

CALLISTO

Callisto has more craters than anything else in our solar system. Its craters are mostly very old, but some newer activity on Callisto's icy surface makes scientists think that there could be an ocean of salt water underneath. Which means that, like Europa, it's possible that Callisto could support life!

IO

Io is covered in volcanoes! It has more volcanic activity than any other place in our solar system. Because Jupiter's gravity is so strong, it pulls on the surface of Io, creating waves made of solid ground! The eruptions on Io can reach several miles upward, and they can even be seen from Earth using powerful telescopes.

EUROPA

Europa has an icy surface at least 10 miles thick, which most likely covers an enormous ocean made of salt water. If scientists are right about Europa's hidden ocean, it holds twice as much water as all of Earth's oceans combined! Because of all that water, Europa is one of the most likely places in the solar system for discovering life as we know it.

SATURN'S MOONS

MOONS EVERY WHICH WAY

Saturn has 82 moons, and 53 of them are officially confirmed so far. There are tons of variety among Saturn's moons—they take lots of different shapes (for example, Hyperion looks like a sponge!), and they range from being as small as a football stadium to larger than Mercury.

ENCELADUS

Among the most interesting of Saturn's moons is **Enceladus**, which likely hides an ocean of water under its icy surface and also seems to have all the elements necessary to form life as we know it.

TITAN

Saturn's biggest moon, **Titan**, is the only place in our solar system besides Earth that's known to have liquid flowing on its surface. But on Titan, the rivers and lakes aren't made of water— they're made of liquid compounds like methane and ethane! Titan's surface is made of water ice, and it might have a water ocean hiding underneath.

RHEA

Rhea is Saturn's second-largest moon, but it's nowhere near as big as Titan. Its surface features lots of canyons and craters, and it also has at least one **ring** around it! When the Cassini spacecraft found evidence of Rhea's rings in 2008, it was the first time scientists had discovered rings around a moon. Like Iapetus, Rhea is very icy—both moons are probably about one-quarter rock and three-quarters ice!

IAPETUS

Iapetus, Saturn's third-largest moon, is unusual because its two hemispheres reflect light very differently: one is extremely dark and the other is much brighter. Scientists aren't certain why that is, but it might have to do with Iapetus's very slow rotation. Some parts face the Sun for long enough that the different hemispheres might have wildly different temperatures. It might also be that the dark part of Iapetus is covered with dust that flies off another moon, Phoebe.

URANUS'S MOONS

SHAKESPEAREAN SATELLITES

Uranus's moons have an unusual distinction: they're the most well-read moons! That's because most of them are named after characters from William Shakespeare's plays. Five of Uranus's moons are bigger than the rest, and there's also a group of eight smaller moons that are so close together that scientists don't know why they don't crash into each other. Uranus has 27 moons altogether, and they make up a unique cast of characters.

William Shakespeare

TITANIA

OBERON

UMBRIEL

MIRANDA

ARIEL

There's **Miranda**, which features giant canyons that go 12 times as deep as Earth's Grand Canyon. There's **Umbriel**, which is ancient and very dark—except for a mysterious bright spot on one side. There's **Titania**, which is Uranus's largest moon and was named for the queen of the fairies in *A Midsummer Night's Dream.* And don't forget **Ariel**, the brightest of Uranus's moons and probably the youngest.

Neptune's Moons

DARK AND MYSTERIOUS

Neptune has 14 moons in all, and they're an odd bunch. Many of them are dark compared to most other objects in our solar system, and because they're so far away, they're more mysterious to us than moons closer to Earth. **Triton** is the largest, and it has ice volcanoes that shoot liquid chemicals into the air—the chemicals immediately freeze and become snow! There's also **Proteus**, which has an odd lumpy shape, and **Nereid**, which has the most irregular orbit of any moon as far as scientists know. In fact, several of Neptune's moons have unusual orbits.

PROTEUS   TRITON

Triton is the only large moon that has an orbit in the opposite direction of its planet's rotation. That's called a **retrograde orbit**.

Nereid orbits very far from Neptune. It takes almost a full Earth year for Nereid to complete one orbit! Many moons have circular orbits, but not Nereid—it's much farther from Neptune at one end of its orbit than at the other end.

Neso and Psamathe are tiny moons with similar orbits. Their orbits take them farther away from their planet than almost any other moons in our solar system. They orbit so far from Neptune that it takes them 26 Earth years to complete one orbit!

PLUTO'S MOONS

FABULOUS FIVE

Pluto—which is now classified as a **dwarf planet**—has just five moons. Scientists think that all five were formed at the same time, when Pluto smashed into some other object in the **Kuiper Belt** very early in the history of the solar system. Four of Pluto's moons are quite small. **Nix** and **Hydra** were both discovered in 2005 by scientists using the **Hubble Space Telescope**. **Kerberos** and **Styx** are both tiny (possibly less than 10 miles across!), and they were discovered even more recently: Kerberos was discovered in 2011 and Styx was discovered in 2012.

But **Charon** is much bigger—it's almost half the size of Pluto itself! That makes Charon the biggest moon relative to its planet in the entire solar system. In fact, scientists sometimes refer to Pluto and Charon as a **double dwarf planet system** rather than calling Charon a moon. So far, scientists don't know of any other double planetary systems in our solar system.

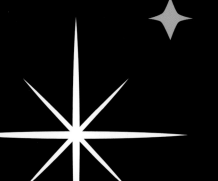

CHARON

NIX

HYDRA

AsteRoiDS, Comets, AnD meteoRS

ANCIENT ARTIFACTS AND COSMIC SNOWBALLS

Asteroids are bits of rock that have been around since our solar system formed over 4 billion years ago. Comets—which some scientists call "cosmic snowballs"—are clumps of space dust and gas that start to burn when they get close to the Sun.

ASTEROIDS

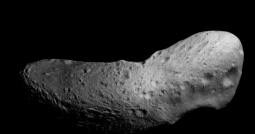

101955 Bennu

Eros

Vesta

There are almost 1 million known asteroids so far, and most of them are part of a giant asteroid belt that orbits the Sun between Mars and Jupiter. Asteroids come in lots of different sizes, from ones that could fit in your house to ones hundreds of miles in diameter. Scientists often study specific asteroids. For instance, scientists have sent a spacecraft to an asteroid called 101955 Bennu, where it will gather samples that could give us insight into the history of life on Earth. Bennu got its name in 2013, but not from scientists—it was named by a nine-year-old who won a contest!

COMETS

As comets orbit the Sun, burning gas and dust fly off them, making beautiful tails that we can sometimes see in the sky. There are over 3,000 comets identified so far.

- **Halley's Comet** passes close enough to see from Earth about once every 75 years. Historical records show observations of Halley's Comet dating back more than 2,000 years.

- **'Oumuamua** was the first confirmed interstellar visitor to our solar system—that means it originally came from a different star! Its name is a Hawaiian word that means: "A messenger from afar arriving first."

- **19P/Borrelley** looks just like a chicken leg!

METEOROIDS, METEORS, AND METEORITES

SPACE ROCKS

These three kinds of space rocks are actually all the *same* space rocks—just at different times! Here's how to tell the difference between them:

Meteoroids are essentially rocks floating in space, whether tiny or large.

Sometimes, meteoroids fly through a planet's atmosphere and burn up, which makes them **meteors**—also called fireballs or shooting stars.

If a meteor makes it all the way to the surface of the planet, then it becomes a **meteorite**!

Beyond our solar system:

all about asterisms and constellations

FIND PICTURES IN THE STARS!

The Sun is the key to life on Earth and the heart of our solar system. But remember, the Sun is actually much like any other star—and there are countless other stars in the universe! Think of it this way: our home galaxy (the **Milky Way Galaxy**) contains at least 100 billion stars. And the universe might contain 100 billion *galaxies*. That means billions and billions of stars! Just like our Sun, many stars have their own planets, so the number of worlds in the universe is truly enormous.

For thousands of years, humans have looked at the stars and seen **asterisms**. Asterisms are groups of stars that appear in a pattern, and they are often said to look like images from the mythologies of various cultures around the world. Outside of science, asterisms are often called **constellations**. Astronomers use the word "constellation" to mean a specific part of the sky, whether or not they're talking about an asterism.

Today, astronomers recognize 88 constellations! The asterisms within those constellations are visible in different parts of the world at different times of the year, but most of them can be seen without a telescope. Try looking for some of these asterisms in the night sky where you live!

THe STaRS

ARieS

THE RAM

Aries is one of the 12 constellations in the **zodiac**, which is the part of the sky that the Sun seems to move through over the course of a year. Its name comes from Greek mythology, and it is one of many asterisms that have been recognized by humans since ancient times. Today, Aries is represented as a ram, but it has been interpreted different ways throughout history. Some records indicate that in ancient Egypt, Aries was seen as an image of Amun-Ra—a god who looked like a man with the head of a ram!

canis MaJoR

THE BIG DOG

In Latin, Canis Major's name spells out exactly what it represents: a big dog! Specifically, it's said to be one of the two hunting dogs that belong to Orion, the hunter asterism. Canis Major contains **Sirius**, the brightest star in our entire night sky! Sirius, which is also known as the dog star, is so bright because it's especially close to our solar system. A star called **VY Canis Majoris**, one of the biggest known stars, is also part of Canis Major.

Canis Minor

THE LITTLE DOG

You guessed it: in Latin, Canis Minor means "lesser dog." Like Canis Major, this constellation is usually seen as a hunting dog following Orion. Sometimes, Canis Minor is said to represent a different dog from Greek mythology: Maera, a dog that was legendary for being faithful to its master. **Procyon**, the brightest star in Canis Minor, is also one of the brightest stars in the sky.

Cassiopeia

THE QUEEN

Cassiopeia looks like a capital letter *W* in the northern summer sky. But sometimes the *W* looks like it's upsidedown. According to Greek mythology, that's because Cassiopeia was a queen who thought she was more beautiful than the children of the gods. Her punishment for being so vain was to hang upside down some of the time!

CentaURUS

THE CENTAUR

Centaurus is a centaur—a Greek mythological creature with the body of a horse and the head and chest of a man. Centaurus is home to the **Alpha Centauri system**, which contains the three stars that are our nearest neighbors in the whole universe. The smallest one is closest to our Sun, and it's called **Proxima Centauri**. The stars of Alpha Centauri are hard to see in the Northern Hemisphere, but farther south, they shine very brightly in the summer sky.

Leo

THE LION

Leo is a lion! It has lots of bright stars, so it's often easy to see in the Northern Hemisphere. In particular, the stars that outline the lion's shoulders and mane form a shape that looks like a backward question mark. Leo was recognized by ancient people long before many other asterisms, and many different cultures called it "lion" in their own languages. Leo is another of the constellations in the **zodiac**. It is also home to a notable **meteor shower** called the **Leonids**, which puts on its bright, colorful show each November.

LYRA

THE LYRE

Lyra is said to represent a lyre, which is a small stringed instrument. Lyra is one of the smaller constellations, but also one of the most interesting! It contains **Vega**, which is the fifth-brightest star in the night sky. Other than the Sun, Vega was also the first star ever photographed! Lyra is also home to the **Ring Nebula**, which is a famous **planetary nebula**. A nebula forms when a star pushes out a bright layer of gas.

ORION

THE HUNTER

For many people, Orion is the star of the stars! It's located right around the equator, which means it can be seen throughout the world. Orion is named after a famed hunter from Greek mythology, and it has been recognized by different names in many cultures throughout recorded history. The three bright stars in a row that often represent the hunter's belt are especially recognizable. Additionally, Orion contains two of the brightest stars in our night sky, **Rigel** and **Betelgeuse** (often pronounced "beetle juice"!).

URSA MAJOR

THE BIG BEAR

Ursa Major's name in Latin means "great bear," and it lives up to that name—Ursa Major is the third-largest constellation in our entire night sky. Seven of its stars form perhaps the most famous asterism: the **Big Dipper**, which looks like the kind of ladle you might use to serve soup. Sometimes, the Big Dipper is also said to represent other objects, like a plough or a wagon. Ursa Major is also important in navigation, because the tip of the bear's tail (or the handle of the ladle!) points toward the **North Star**.

URSA MINOR

THE LITTLE BEAR

Ursa Minor is the "little bear" to Ursa Major's "great bear," and it also has a group of stars that looks like a ladle. Those stars are known as the **Little Dipper**. Ursa Minor is much smaller than Ursa Major, but it's just as important: its brightest star is **Polaris**, which is also known as the North Star. Polaris is actually a system of three stars close together, and they're known as the North Star because they're in the part of the sky that's right above Earth's North Pole. Especially for sailors (or anyone trying to figure out directions!), finding Polaris is one sure way of knowing which way is north.

GALAXIES

BILLIONS UPON BILLIONS OF GALAXIES

Our solar system is just one part of another enormous system in space: a galaxy!
There are so many galaxies in the universe that we can't even come close to counting
them all yet—there may be as many as 100 billion! And each galaxy contains billions of stars.
Galaxies are held together by gravity, and they're made of dust and gas as well as all the stars
and their solar systems—planets, moons, space rocks, all of it! In between the galaxies, the universe is
just huge expanses of empty space.

THE MILKY WAY

The Milky Way is our home! It contains our Sun and our solar system, plus billions of other stars. When you look up at the night sky, the other stars you see are all part of the Milky Way, and most of them have their own planets, too. The Milky Way looks like a giant spiral pinwheel, with four arms stretching away from the center. It's one of a cluster of about 30 galaxies called the **Local Group**. The Milky Way got its name because people looking at the sky long ago thought that the pattern it makes in our sky looks like a flowing road made of milk. In very dark places, you can sometimes see those milky streaks in the night sky yourself!

Most of the Milky Way looks bright from Earth, but there's also a dark band in the middle of its whitish bands. That dark area is what's often called the **Great Rift**. Scientists think that it is made of up clouds of dust that block Earth's view of part of the Milky Way. It's likely that new stars are forming within those dust clouds! Some ancient cultures in South America even saw patterns and images in the dark areas of the Milky Way. These images are now known as "dark cloud constellations."

GALACTIC NEIGHBORS

Andromeda is the Milky Way's nearest neighboring galaxy! It's in the Local Group, the same group of galaxies where the Milky Way is located. Andromeda is one of the most massive galaxies in the group, along with the Milky Way itself. Scientists think that in about four billion years, Andromeda could collide with the Milky Way. But because galaxies are so enormous and hold so much empty space, even having the edges of the two bumping together might not cause a commotion; the stars and planets could just glide right by each other. Like the Milky Way (and about two-thirds of all known galaxies), Andromeda is a spiral galaxy. Sometimes, it's even possible to see Andromeda from Earth without a telescope!

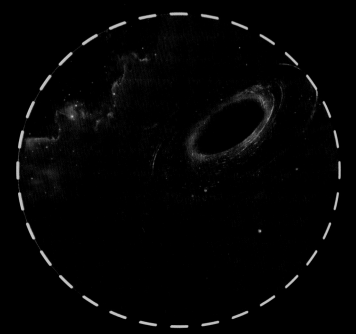

BLACK HOLES

Black holes sound mysterious, but really, they're just spots where a whole lot of matter is packed very tightly together in a small space. But because of all that matter, black holes have a LOT of gravity! In fact, their gravitational pull is so strong that nothing that gets close to a black hole can get away—not even light, which is why they appear to be completely dark.

You wouldn't want to get close to a black hole; they're so strong that they can rip apart an entire star. But at the same time, our whole existence may depend on them—specifically, on the one supermassive black hole at the center of our very own galaxy! All the stars in the Milky Way orbit this one enormous black hole, but scientists don't know which came first, the black hole or the galaxy. Don't worry, though—Earth is far enough from the black hole at the center of the Milky Way that we won't be sucked into it.

EXPLORING SPACE

SPACECRAFT

When humans set out to explore space, spacecraft help them do it! Spacecraft are machines that can be anything from small probes to huge space shuttles. Sometimes they're robots that head out on their own, and sometimes they're vehicles that carry astronauts inside them! Usually, spacecraft need rockets to launch them into space. Here are just a few of the many important spacecraft that NASA has launched over the years:

APOLLO SPACECRAFT

The Apollo program was NASA's first program for sending humans to the moon! The first Apollo flight was in 1968 and the last one was in 1972. The earlier flights tested the spacecraft and other equipment, and the later flights carried astronauts to the moon. The astronauts rode in a spacecraft called the Apollo Command Module, and they used another spacecraft, the Lunar Module, to land on the moon once they got there. Apollo 11 in July 1969 was the first mission in all of human history to land on the moon. During the Apollo program, 12 astronauts in total walked on the moon. They studied what they saw and brought samples of moon rocks back to Earth for the first time!

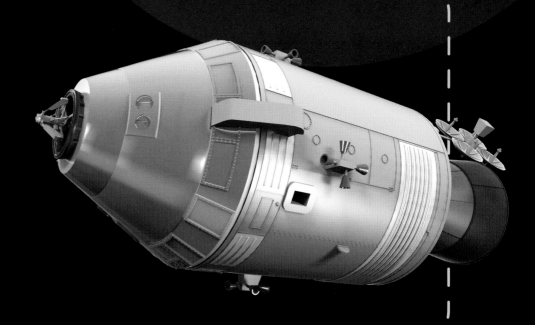

VOYAGER 1 AND VOYAGER 2

Voyager 1 and Voyager 2 are robotic probes that NASA launched into space in 1977. They were originally set to explore Jupiter and Saturn, but they didn't stop there! They've both been flying through space for over 40 years, and they still send data about the far reaches of space back to scientists on Earth. Voyager 2 flew by Uranus and Neptune—it's the only spacecraft that has ever visited those far-off worlds.

Today, both Voyager 1 and Voyager 2 are exploring interstellar space at the far edges of our solar system, and they're both over 10 billion miles from the Sun.

The Voyager probes won't ever return to Earth. But using a giant radio system called the Deep Space Network, they have sent all kinds of important information back to Earth. For instance, they've found details about Saturn's rings and evidence of volcanoes on Jupiter's moon Io. Both Voyager 1 and Voyager 2 carry copies of what's called the Golden Record, which is a record holding music and sounds from Earth, as well as pictures and scientific data about our home. If the Voyager probes ever run into any alien civilizations, the records will be our message of life on Earth!

OPPORTUNITY AND SPIRIT

Opportunity and Spirit are twin spacecraft that NASA launched in 2003 to explore Mars. They're both rovers, which means that they're robots that drive around on the surface of Mars! Spirit got stuck in Martian dirt and ended its mission in 2011, and NASA stayed in touch with Opportunity all the way until 2018, when a dust storm blocked communications. During their time exploring Mars, Opportunity and Spirit sent back huge amounts of information to NASA, including evidence that Mars seemed to have liquid water a long time ago and could have supported life as we know it.

INSIGHT

InSight is a Mars lander that's currently out exploring the planet. InSight is looking for information about the inside of Mars! It does this by tracking the geological activity (like earthquakes) on Mars, as well as the planet's temperature and the meteorites that hit it. Like other rocky planets, Mars has layers under its surface called the crust, mantle, and core. By finding information about these layers on Mars, InSight can help scientists understand how rocky planets—including Earth!—formed and became the planets we know today.

CASSINI SPACECRAFT

Cassini was a spacecraft that NASA (working with scientists in Europe) sent into orbit around Saturn. Cassini orbited Saturn for more than 10 years and sent scientists tons of data about Saturn, its rings, and its many moons. It also brought along a probe called Huygens, which it dropped onto Titan, Saturn's largest moon. Huygens's landing was the first time that humans ever landed an object on a moon other than Earth's moon! The images that Cassini sent back to Earth are some of the most stunning pictures of our solar system. In 2017, the mission ended when Cassini left Saturn's orbit and burned up in the planet's atmosphere, which scientists planned so that Cassini would not hit any of Saturn's moons when it ran out of fuel.

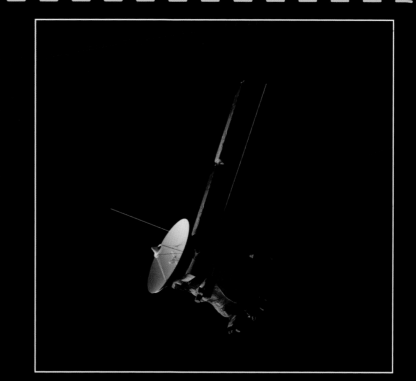

THE HUBBLE SPACE TELESCOPE

The Hubble Space Telescope is an extremely powerful telescope that orbits around Earth, capturing images of space and sending them back to scientists on Earth. Some of the images Hubble has made are of galaxies billions of light-years away! That means that the light from those galaxies took billions of years to reach Hubble. NASA launched Hubble in 1990, and today it's used by astronomers all over the world to study our universe. Hubble has taught us so much of what we know about space: it has shown us images of countless faraway galaxies, helped scientists discover dark energy, and provided evidence that the universe is over 13 billion years old. Who knows what Hubble might reveal in the future!

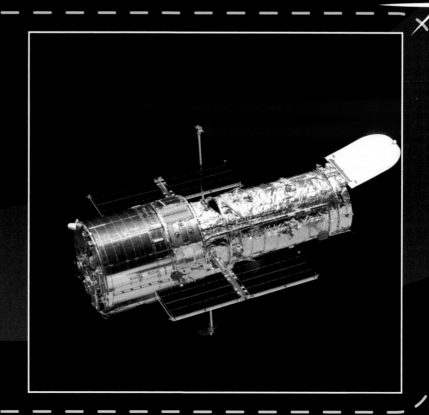

THE INTERNATIONAL SPACE STATION

The International Space Station is one of the key tools in our exploration of space. It is a large spacecraft orbiting Earth, and different groups of astronauts have been living there since the year 2000! The International Space Station has a few different purposes:

- **It's a home to several astronauts!** It can support a crew of six people at a time.

- **It's a scientific laboratory!** Through the astronauts who live and work there, scientists can learn more about space and what it's like to live there. Eventually, this may help scientists send humans even farther into space.

- **It's a way of teaming up with other countries!** Scientists from several nations around the world worked together to build the International Space Station, and it is still shared between them today.

The International Space Station is important, but it's not especially big; it's only about the size of a football field. But it's fast in its orbit around Earth—it makes one complete orbit in only an hour and a half!

ROCKETS

When it comes to exploring space, rockets do the heavy lifting! They burn powerful fuel to launch all kinds of things into space—including satellites, supplies for the **International Space Station**, and spacecraft heading out to explore other worlds. Rockets also launch astronauts into space during NASA missions! Usually, rockets create clouds of gas when they burn fuel, and that gas is what pushes the rocket forward through space.

SATURN V

One of the most famous rockets is **Saturn V**, which NASA used to send astronauts to the moon during the **Apollo program**. It was taller than the Statue of Liberty, and it was extremely powerful. Saturn V could launch the weight of about four school buses all the way to the moon! There were many different Saturn V rockets built over the years. The last one launched in 1973, and it carried the Skylab space station into Earth's orbit. Today, scientists continue to develop more and more powerful rockets all the time.

Ready in 3 . . . 2 . . . 1 . . . liftoff! Space shuttles like this one launch astronauts into outer space.

Looking For Life out There

Given how enormous the universe is, lots of scientists think that there must be life of some kind beyond Earth. That's right—aliens could be real! But if they are, what are they like? Where are they, and how do we find them? These are questions that scientists are working hard to answer. Right now, tools like the Hubble Space Telescope and probes exploring the far reaches of space are looking for information about any signs of life that might be out there.

When scientists talk about finding life, they often mean finding what's called "life as we know it"—that is, creatures that have cells and that rely on familiar things like water and oxygen in order to survive. In other words, creatures a lot like the living things on Earth! But it's also possible that space could hold life as we *don't* know it. It could be that in faraway worlds, life has evolved in ways that we can't even imagine. So when we do find alien life, it might not look anything like we've ever expected!

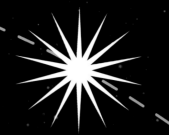

Right now, scientists are focusing on a few likely targets in the search for life beyond Earth:

- **Mars:** Our neighboring planet probably doesn't hold any life today. But living things may have lived there in the past, since there's some evidence that there used to be liquid water on Mars. NASA has plans to launch a new rover to look for more evidence—and maybe even alien fossils!

- **Europa:** Because Jupiter's moon Europa probably has an ocean of liquid water underneath its icy surface, it's one of the places most likely to be home to life as we know it. Within the next few years, NASA will launch a new spacecraft called **Clipper** to explore Europa further! Titan, Saturn's biggest moon, is another possibility in our solar system.

- **Exoplanets:** Exoplanets are planets that orbit other stars rather than our own Sun. There are hundreds of billions of exoplanets in the Milky Way, our home galaxy, so scientists are working on building powerful telescopes that can fly to outer space and search those distant worlds for signs of life! One of them, the James Webb Space Telescope, has a launch date of 2021.

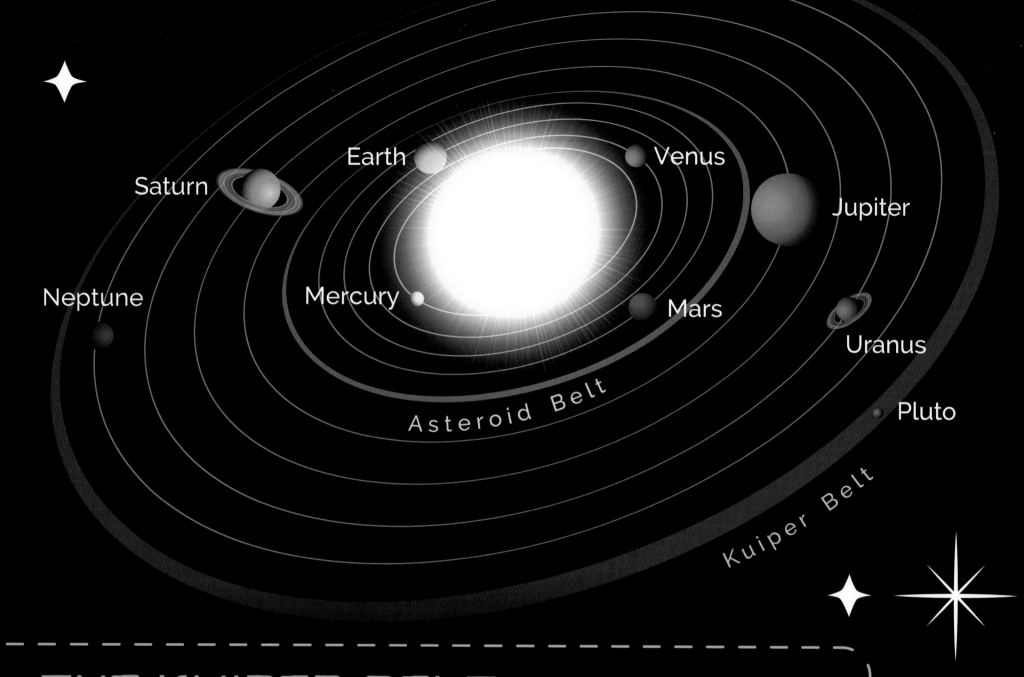

THE KUIPER BELT

The Kuiper Belt is a doughnut-shaped region in our solar system that is very far away from Earth. It's located way out past Neptune, and it's full of ancient, icy objects of many different shapes and sizes—from tiny comets to dwarf planets! The dwarf planets Pluto, Haumea, Makemake, and Eris are all in the Kuiper Belt.

The Kuiper Belt is also home to a small, icy space object named Arrokoth that looks like a red snowman, which scientists learned about when the spacecraft New Horizons flew by it in 2019. Arrokoth's name comes from a Native American word that means "sky" in the Powhatan/Algonquian language—which makes sense, since it's the farthest-away object that humans have ever explored up close!

THE OORT CLOUD

The Oort Cloud is even farther away from Earth than the Kuiper Belt. It's all the way at the far edge of our solar system, and it's thought to be shaped like a giant bubble that creates a shell around the entire solar system. No spacecraft from Earth have ever visited the Oort Cloud, so scientists have never looked at it directly. Instead, scientists have learned about the Oort Cloud from comets that seem to have come from it.

The Oort Cloud is made up of countless icy objects, some as big as mountains—or bigger! And the Oort Cloud is so far away that even the spacecraft Voyager 1—which travels about 1 million miles every day!—won't reach the closest edge of the Oort Cloud for at least 300 years.

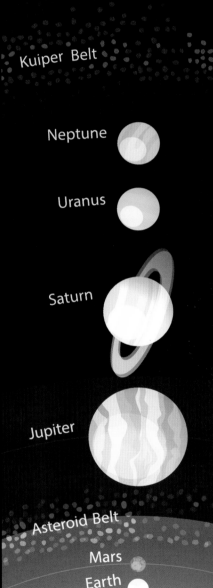

Oort Cloud

Kuiper Belt

Neptune

Uranus

Saturn

Jupiter

Asteroid Belt

Mars

Earth

Venus

Mercury

DaRK MaTTeR

5%
Matter

27%
Dark Matter

68%
Dark Energy

Dark matter is one of space's greatest mysteries. No one yet knows exactly what it is, it's invisible, and scientists haven't been able to study it directly. So how do we know it exists? The answer is complex, but essentially scientists studied certain aspects of the universe—including the gravity that pulls on light from faraway stars, the movements of galaxies, and particular kinds of radiation—and realized that there must be much more mass in the universe than what we can observe directly. It's a little bit like looking at the shadow of something and trying to figure out what that thing is! All that extra mass is dark matter. Even though we don't know what it is, scientists estimate that dark matter makes up about **27%** of the universe.

Some scientists have theories about what dark matter might be. A few possibilities include:

- **Brown dwarfs**, which are stars that never became big enough to start burning

- **White dwarfs**, which are leftover cores from dead stars

- **Black holes or neutron stars**, which are left when especially large stars explode

- **Something else altogether!** It could be that dark matter is made of particles that scientists don't even know about yet.

There's also another mystery called dark energy. We know about the existence of dark energy because images from the Hubble Space Telescope revealed that the universe is expanding faster all the time—we just don't know *why* that is. Whatever is causing the universe to expand is what scientists call dark energy. Scientists think that dark energy might make up as much as 68% of the universe. That means that matter we can observe—planets, moons, stars, and nearly everything mentioned in this book!—is really only about 5% of what the universe contains.

GLOSSARY

SPACE-TALK CAN SOUND CONFUSING, BUT HAVING A FEW DEFINITIONS HANDY MAKES THINGS A LOT EASIER. HERE'S YOUR GUIDE TO THE WORDS AND PHRASES BUDDING ASTRONAUTS NEED TO KNOW.

asteroid
A bit of rock floating through space. Asteroids have been around ever since our solar system formed.

astronaut
A person who goes out to explore space in a spacecraft.

astronomer
A kind of scientist who studies space.

atmosphere
The layers of gas that surround Earth and other planets. They're held there by gravity.

axis
The imaginary line through the center of a planet. Think of it like this: if a planet were an apple, the axis would be the core! All planets rotate on an axis, which means that they spin in place with the axis in the middle.

black hole
A spot in space where a lot of matter is packed together into a small space. Because they have so much mass, black holes also have an enormous amount of gravity.

comet
A clump of space dust and gas that starts to burn when it gets close to the Sun.

constellation
A specific part of the night sky. Sometimes, you'll also hear this word used to refer to *asterisms*—groups of stars that appear to form a pattern in the sky.

crater
A large dent in the ground. They're usually shaped like a bowl and can be caused
by an explosion or something very large hitting the ground.

dark matter
A mysterious kind of mass that makes up about 27% of the universe. Scientists don't know what dark matter is yet.

galaxy
A group of stars and their solar systems. Each galaxy is home to billions of stars, and
gravity holds them all together. Our own galaxy is called the Milky Way.

gas
One of the three normal phases of matter—the other two are *liquid* and *solid*. In a gas, the molecules
hold together very weakly. That means that a gas will change both its shape and its volume to
match whatever container it is in. For example, mist is water in the form of a gas!

gas giant
A kind of planet that's mostly made out of clouds of gas. Unlike Earth, a gas giant does not have a solid surface that you could
stand on, but it might have a solid core at the center of all that gas. Jupiter and Saturn are the gas giants in our solar system.

gravity
A natural force that pulls things toward each other. Gravity holds together everything in our
solar system, and it even holds together galaxies. But other forces can overcome gravity—
just think, every time you pick up an object, you're doing exactly that!

hemisphere
One of the two halves of a planet like Earth. Imagine a line going around the middle of the planet like a belt—
above that line is the Northern Hemisphere, and below it is the Southern Hemisphere. You could also divide the
planet from top to bottom, and then you would get the Eastern Hemisphere and Western Hemisphere.

ice giant
A kind of planet that's mostly made out of a mixture of icy substances: water, methane, and ammonia.
The "ice" isn't solid like an ice cube, though—it's more like a dense liquid. Ice giants have a small
rocky core at their center. The ice giants in our solar system are Uranus and Neptune.

light-year
A light-year sounds like a stretch of time, but it's actually a way to measure distance. Specifically, a light-year is the distance that light travels during one year. One light-year equals 5,878,499,810,000 miles!

liquid
One of the three normal phases of matter—the other two are *gas* and *solid*. In a liquid, the molecules hold together somewhat weakly. That means that a liquid will always stay the same volume, but it will usually change its shape depending on the container it is in. For example, rain is water in a liquid form!

mass
The amount of matter that makes up something. Put simply, something with a large mass has a lot of stuff in it!

matter
The stuff everything is made up of. You're made of matter, and so are the cells that make up your body—and so are the atoms that make up your cells! Everything else in the solar system is made of matter, too.

meteor
A meteoroid that has flown thrown a planet's atmosphere and burned up. Meteors are also called *shooting stars*.

meteorite
A meteor that has fallen to the surface of Earth or another planet.

meteoroid
A rock floating in space. They can be all different sizes, from tiny to enormous.

moon
An object in space that orbits a planet or another big object, like a dwarf planet or an asteroid. Earth has one moon—that's what we usually mean when we say "the Moon"—but there are many more across our solar system. Scientists often call moons "satellites."

NASA
NASA stands for National Aeronautics and Space Administration. NASA is the part of the United States government that is in charge of science and technology related to airplanes and space.

orbit
The curved path that an object takes through space as it moves around another object. For example, the Moon orbits Earth, and the Earth orbits the Sun.

planet
A very large object in a solar system. There are eight planets in our solar system. Planets orbit their suns, are sphere-shaped, and are the only large objects near their orbits. *Dwarf planets* are also sphere-shaped objects that orbit their suns, but they are not the only large objects near their orbits.

rotation
The movement of an object in space spinning around its axis. The rotation of the Earth from west to east is what creates the change from day to night and back again!

rover
A kind of spacecraft that lands of the surface of a planet or other object in space. Rovers are usually robots with wheels that look a bit like cars!

solar system
The collection of everything (planets, moons, and more!) that orbits around a particular star, plus the star itself. In our solar system, the Sun is that star.

solid
One of the three normal phases of matter—the other two are *gas* and *liquid*. In a solid, the molecules hold together strongly. That means that a solid always stays the same volume and the same shape, no matter what container it is in. For example, an ice cube is water in a solid form!

spacecraft
A machine created by humans to explore and study space. Spacecraft can be relatively small, like a satellite or a rover, or they can be as enormous as a space shuttle.

star
A huge ball of hot gas that's held together by its own gravity. Stars are mostly made out of hydrogen and helium. Our Sun is a star!

telescope
A tool that humans use to look into the sky or into space. Telescopes can be small, like one you might find in a toy store, or enormous—like the Hubble Space Telescope! Telescopes use mirrors and lenses to make faraway objects look closer to us.

universe
Everything that exists anywhere in space or time. Solar systems, galaxies, all kinds of matter—the universe is truly *everything*!

How to Sticker Your Room

STEP 1:

Check out the chart on the opposite page to see how far apart you should place your stickers. If you follow the chart, you'll be able to make your own miniature version of the same distances that exist between the objects in our solar system! You can also ask a parent or another adult to help you.

STEP 2:

Now, pick spots for your stickers! To make sure you get them just where you want them, you can mark spots on your wall with an erasable pencil to remind yourself where each one should go. Start with the heart of our solar system—the Sun! Once you have the Sun ready to go, it will be easier to place your other stickers.

STEP 3:

Next, place the eight planets around the Sun. Again using the chart to guide you, use your stickers to re-create the way the planets really are spaced around the Sun. Then, you can move on to adding the moons and other stickers in their proper places.

STEP 4:

Finish up with the stars. Since the stars are outside our solar system, you can place them wherever you think they look best. Now, step back and admire your work—you did it! Your bedroom is officially a solar system.

A NOTE ON ACCURACY

To re-create the same distances that exist between the real objects in our solar system, you'd need a pretty enormous room—for example, if you put Mercury about 3 inches from the Sun, you'd need to put Pluto over 30 feet away from the Sun! But using the guidelines on page 59, you can still make a miniature version of the solar system that's close to the real thing.

WHERE DOES EVERYTHING GO?

You can use your stickers however you want, but to make your bedroom look similar to the real solar system, follow these simple guidelines for placing your stickers! You don't have to get the measurements perfect—even astronomers use estimates and best guesses to do their work. Just give it a try and use your imagination to fill in the rest!

- **Mercury** should go quite close to the Sun.

- **Venus** should go a little less than twice as far away from the Sun as Mercury. For example, if Mercury is 1 inch away from the Sun, Venus should go a bit less than 2 inches away from the Sun.

- **Earth** should go a bit more than twice as far away from the Sun as Mercury.

- **Mars** should go about one and half times as far away from the Sun as Earth. So, if Earth is 4 inches away from the Sun, Mars should go 6 inches away from the Sun.

- **Jupiter** should go a bit more than 5 times as far away from the Sun as Earth.

- **Saturn** is where your room might start to feel a little small! It should go about twice as far away from the Sun as Jupiter.

- **Uranus** should go even farther! How can you get creative to make your Uranus sticker feel far from your Sun sticker?

- **Neptune** is the farthest of all from the Sun. Can it go in the opposite corner of your room? What about down the hall? Use your imagination!

CARING FOR YOUR STICKERS

- If you don't like where you put your stickers, no problem! You can take them off and stick them back on in a different spot. They won't leave any marks on your walls.

- If you don't want to stick them back up right away, make sure you store them safely inside your book so they don't dry out.

- If your stickers are a little less sticky than they used to be, you can fix that. Just put a tiny bit of water on a soft cloth and gently clean the back of the sticker. Cleaning the part of the wall where you want to put the sticker can also help.

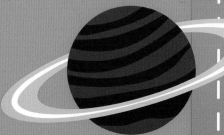

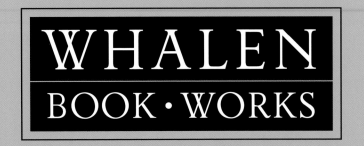

PUBLISHING PRACTICAL & CREATIVE NONFICTION

Whalen Book Works is a small, independent book publishing company based
in Kennebunkport, Maine, that combines top-notch design, unique formats, and
fresh content to create truly innovative gift books.

Our unconventional approach to bookmaking is a close-knit,
creative, and collaborative process among authors, artists, designers,
editors, and booksellers. We publish a small, carefully curated list each season,
and we take the time to make each book exactly what it needs to be.

We believe in giving back. That's why we plant one tree for every ten books sold.
Your purchase supports a tree in the Rocky Mountain National Park.

Get in touch!

Visit us at **Whalenbooks.com**
or write to us at
68 North Street, Kennebunkport, ME 04046

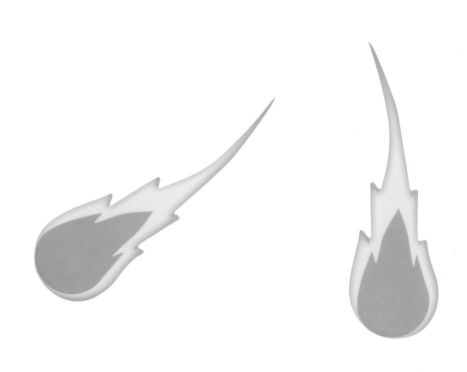

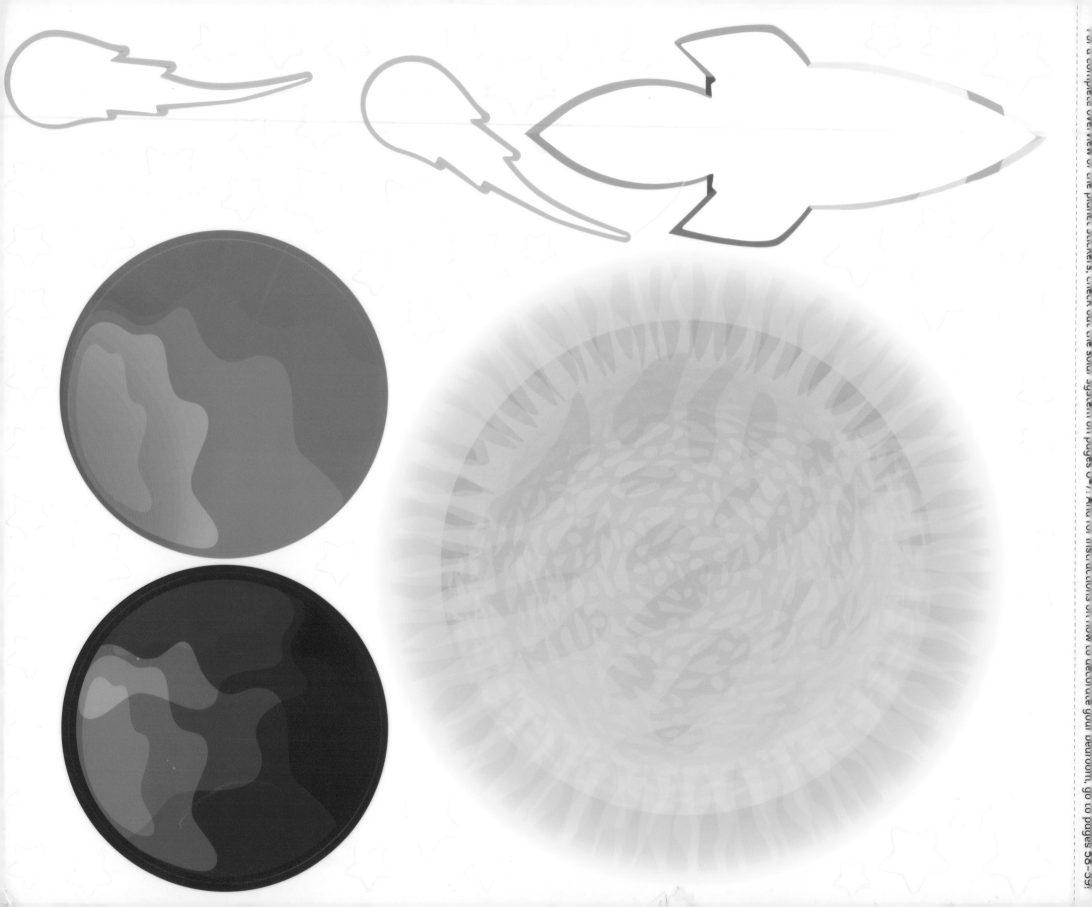

For a complete overview of the planet stickers, check out the solar system on pages 6–7! And for instructions on how to decorate your bedroom, go to pages 58–59.